EARPLUG *Erotica*

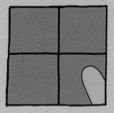

BY MIKE McCOY

SANTA
MONICA
PRESS

Published by: Santa Monica Press LLC
P.O. Box 850
Solana Beach, CA 92075
1-800-784-9553
www.santamonicapress.com
books@santamonicapress.com

S A N T A
M O N I C A
P R E S S

Printed in Canada

Santa Monica Press books are available at special quantity discounts when purchased in bulk by corporations, organizations, or groups. Please call our Special Sales department at 1-800-784-9553.

ISBN-13 978-1-59580-104-3

Cover and interior design and production by Future Studio

The Sauna

Climbers

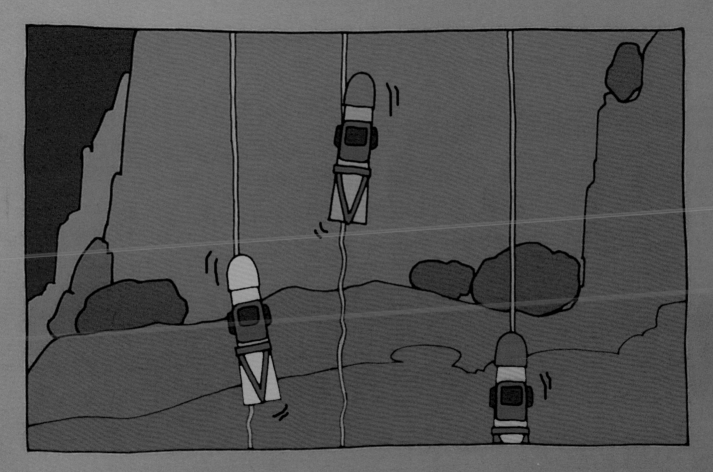

Skydivers

The Island

House Party

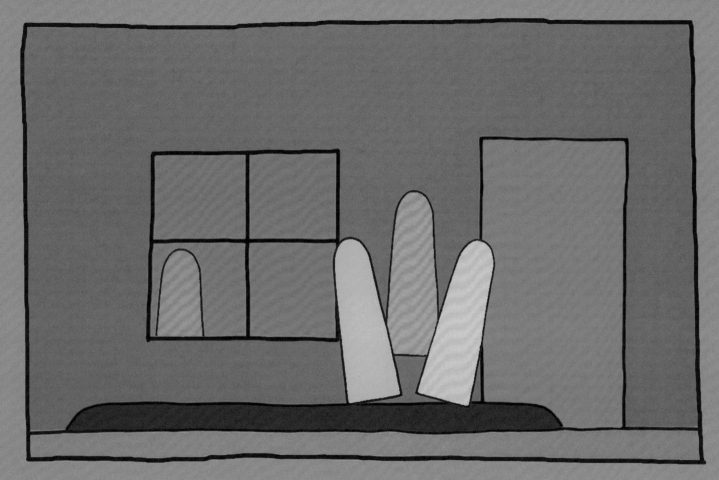

Campers

CAMPING

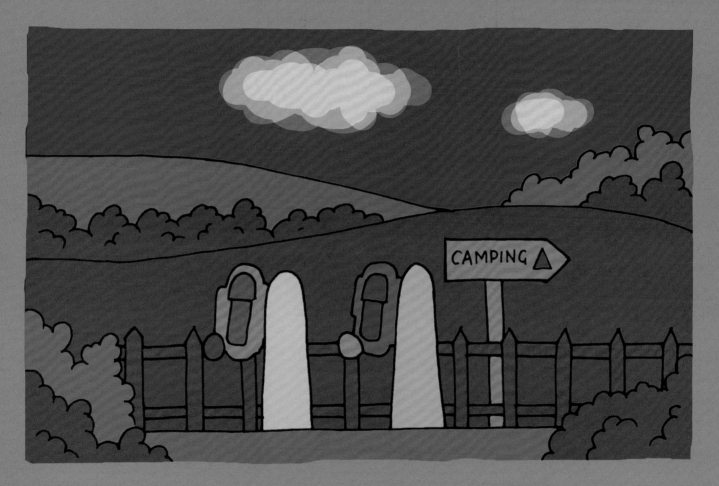

Scuba Divers

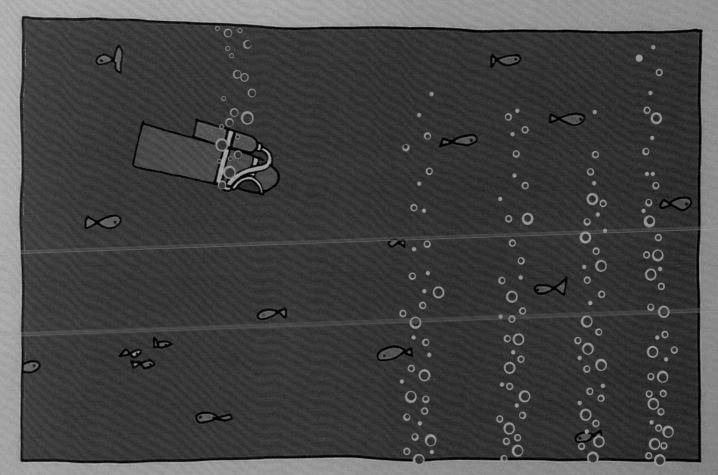

The Office

OFFICE
CONDUCT

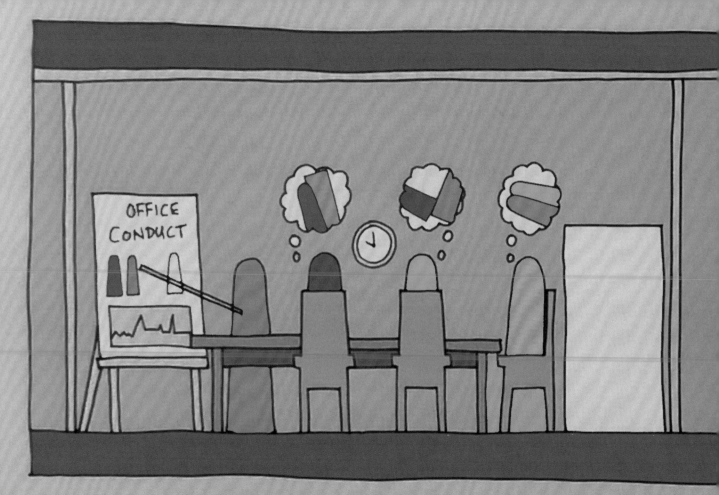

COFFEE
FOTO COPY

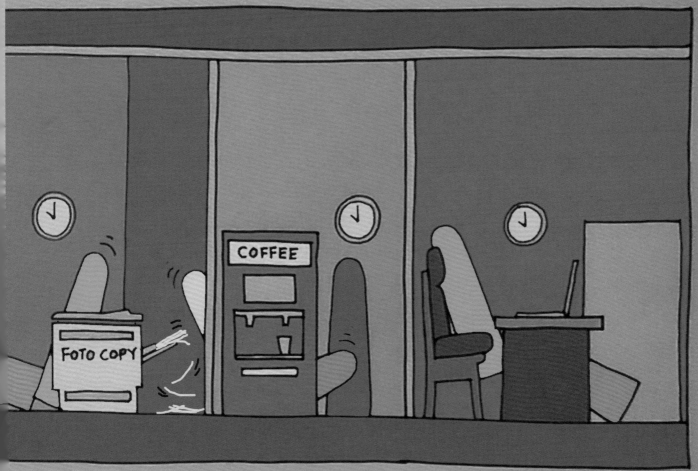

The Visitor

Dinner Party

The Club

ENTRY
!

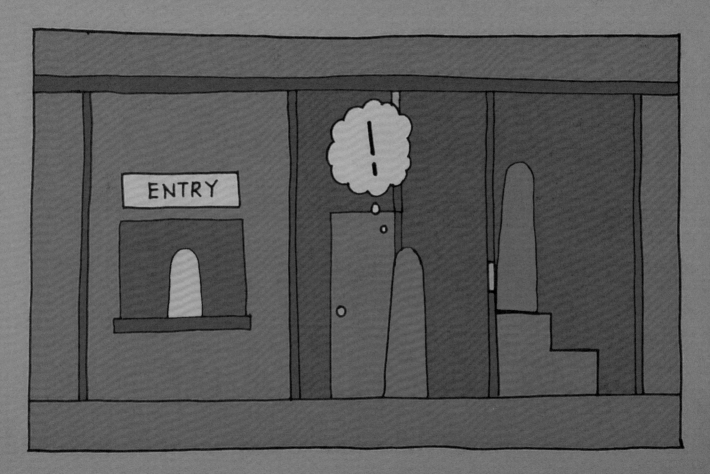

The Warehouse

Walking the Dog

Zero G

Recreation room
G

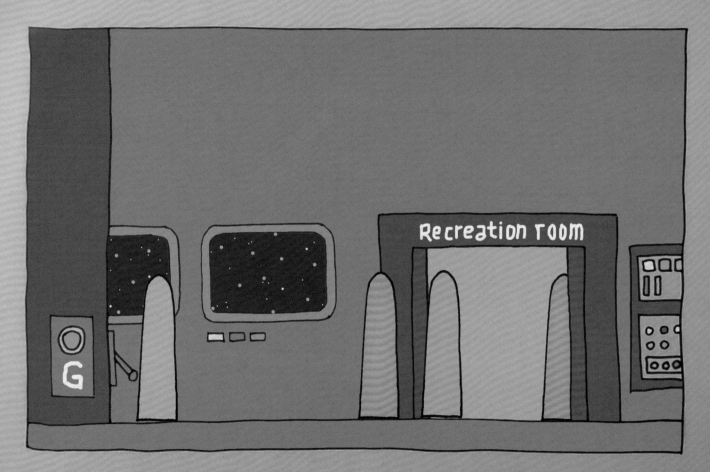

R eation ro
G

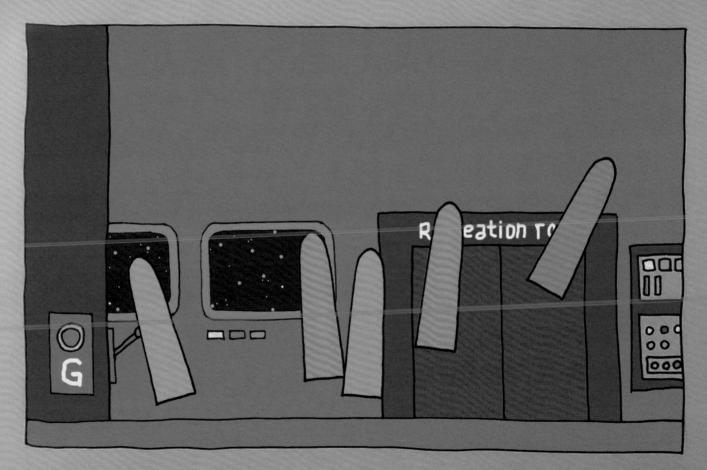

room
G

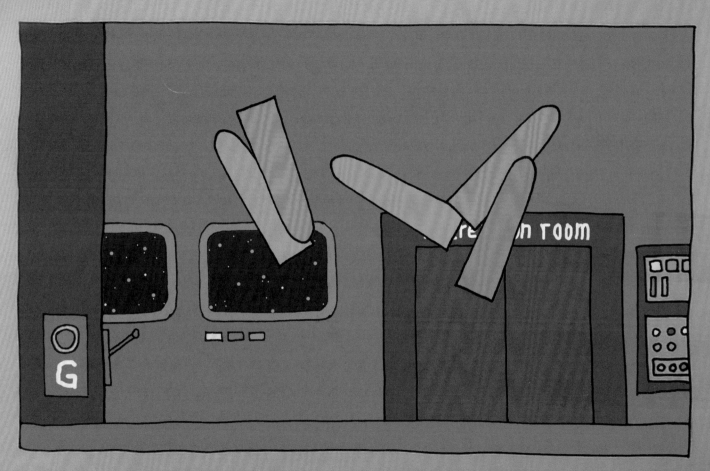

Recreation
G

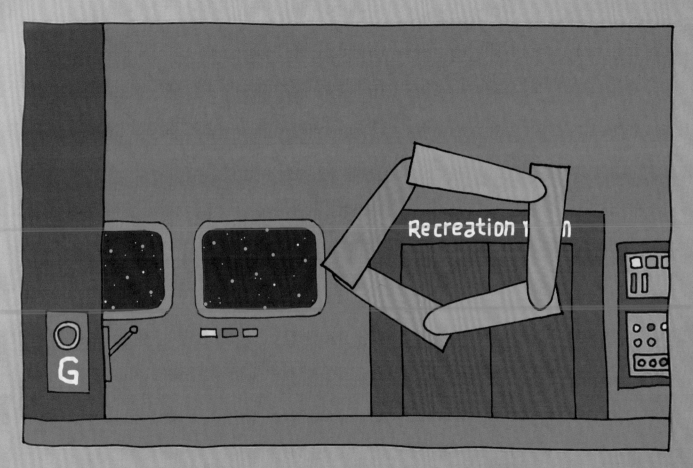